HOW THEY WORK

M1 ABRAMS
Main Battle Tank

FRANK VANN

MALLARD
PRESS

A dramatic night shot
of an M1 105mm
salvo.

Contents

The Development of
the Battle Tank   6

Weaponry and
Ammunition   16

Armour   23

The M1 Abrams
Battle Tank   26

Index   46

Above: The low profile of the Abrams M1A1 Tank and its shallow gun turret are shown to good advantage in this side view. The two machine guns on the top of the turret are used against aircraft and lighter targets.

Right: If this were the first sight that an enemy had of the Abrams M1A1 Battle Tank, he could not fail to realize that he was faced with a formidable opponent. The low outline of the turret is again obvious. Its sloping front is designed to deflect enemy fire.

The Development of the Battle Tank

At the end of the last century, opposing armies still attempted to attack each other with firearms standing square on at relatively close quarters. A major problem of this form of engagement was that, in order to get near enough to each other, the soldiers had to cross an open battlefield swept by cannon fire, with horrendous results. The advent and use of the machine-gun at this time made the casualties even worse.

During World War I, in the early years of this century, trench warfare was used for the first time. Instead of repelling an enemy attack by advancing to meet him in the open, it was found more effective to lie in wait in a system of trenches dug into the ground. If the enemy advanced for an attack, the defending troops would shelter in their trenches until the enemy was near enough to be assailed with rifle or machine-gun fire.

Because of these tactics, it became horrifyingly expensive in terms of casualties to attempt an attack on the enemy positions. The result was a stalemate. Any attempts to pierce the enemy lines by direct assault with infantry soldiers resulted in hundreds of thousands of casualties in one battle. Usually, the amount of enemy territory captured in such assaults was so small that the price in human lives was seen to be far too high to pay for so little gain. Some way of breaking the stalemate had to be found.

What was needed was a way of transporting an attacking force towards the enemy lines while at the same time protecting it from the hail of bullets which swept across no-man's-land as soon as any movement was detected by the enemy.

Armour plate similar to that used for years on battleships was seen to be one answer to the problem. If a gun could be mounted on a vehicle covered in armour plate, it would be possible to drive the vehicle across no-man's-land up to the enemy lines without its crew being injured by gun-fire. The gun could then be used to kill the enemy troops in their trenches and to break through into the territory behind the enemy lines.

Leonardo da Vinci had produced plans for an armoured fighting vehicle in the 15th century. It consisted of a reinforced dome mounted on wheels. The dome was thick enough to prevent arrows or the relatively ineffective bullets of the time from getting through to the men inside. The idea was that a number of troops would climb inside the dome while it was in their own lines, and would push it on its wheels up to the enemy positions, leap out and attack the enemy at close quarters, having successfully survived the crossing of the open space between the armies,

This photograph taken during World War I shows one of the earliest tanks crossing a trench. The guns mounted in the side turrets were toys compared with the armament of a modern tank. Nevertheless, at the time, they succeeded in breaking through the German lines and ending the stalemate produced by trench warfare.

remaining uninjured because of the protection which the armoured vehicle afforded them.

It was obviously pointless to think of using a wheeled vehicle to cross the battlefield in World War I. The fields of Flanders had been raked by gunfire for three years. The ground was churned up into a vast sea of mud, feet thick. Any wheeled vehicle would sink into the mud and quickly become immobilized. The landscape was also pitted with shell-holes and strewn with felled trees so that, even in dry weather, any conventional wheeled carriage would find it impossible to remain on an even keel as it attempted to cross the desolate landscape.

How then is a vehicle prevented from sinking into the mud? In the case of a tank not much can be done to reduce the mass of the vehicle. That is decided by the mass of the gun and its ammunition, the engine, the armour plate and the crew. The only way to lessen the bearing press-

ure – that is, the weight acting on a unit of area – is to increase the area. For instance, if a vehicle weighs 2,000kg (4,409lb) and the area of contact of its four tyres with the ground is 600cm^2 (93.1sq in), the bearing pressure applied to the ground by the vehicle is about 3.33kg/cm^2 (47.36lb/sq in). That result is obtained by dividing the weight of the vehicle by the area of its tyres in contact with the ground.

If the maximum bearing pressure which the ground is capable of supporting is less than the pressure that the vehicle is applying to the ground, the vehicle will sink. In that case, to prevent the vehicle from getting bogged down, the area of contact has to be increased between the wheels and the ground by some factor. Heavy earth-moving vehicles do this today by using large balloon tyres. At the time of World War I, such balloon tyres did not exist. Even if they had been available, they would not have been of

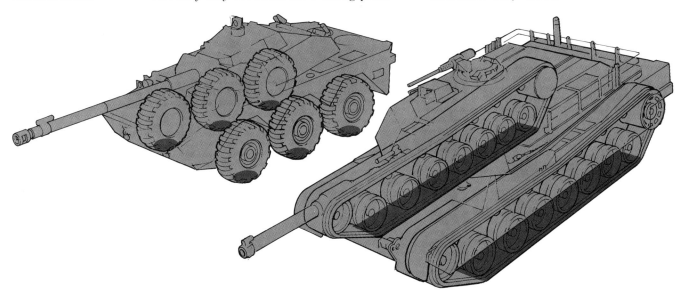

much use on a battlefield where one shot would have punctured them.

The one invention which made the modern tank possible was the caterpillar track which is used not only on tanks but also on agricultural tractors. Like tanks they have to work on soft soil. Basically, the caterpillar track consists of a long belt of hinged metal plates which runs around a series of wheels on the side of the vehicle and which are aligned parallel with the ground. The plates which are in the lower half of the chain all rest on the ground and provide a very large area to support the weight of the vehicle. As a result, the tank or tractor can safely cross very soft soil without sinking in.

Caterpillar tracks also have the advantage that, unlike wheels, they can bridge trenches. If an automobile attempts to drive across even a narrow trench, the front wheels will drop into any gap more than a few inches wide and bring the vehicle to a sudden stop. Because the track of a tank is several feet long from front to back, it can safely cross a trench 2m (6½ft) wide without falling in.

A tank's engine, instead of driving the wheels like those of an automobile, drives sprockets which engage in the tracks and makes them move in a continuous loop around the supporting wheels on each side of the tank. In effect, the tracks are laying a roadway for the tank to run over. As the rear wheels pass over the back end of the track, the used plates are picked up by the rear sprocket, carried forward along the side of the tank and re-laid at the front to be traversed again by the wheels. If you look carefully at a tank when it is moving, you will see that the part of the track which is in contact with the ground is lying still while the tank passes over it.

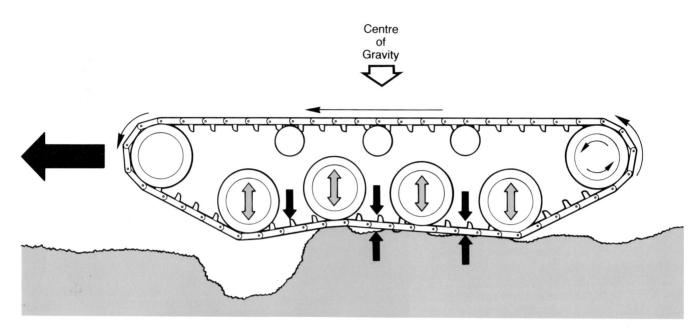

Centre
of
Gravity

Above: Because of the long continuous surface at the bottom of its tracks, a tank finds no difficulty in crossing ditches up to 2m (6½ft) wide. In effect, the tank lays a metal roadway for itself on the ground which it is going to cross. After it has passed over this roadway, it takes it up again and passes it to the front for re-use.

Right: This close-up view of a World War I tank shows the device used to tension the tracks. Rotating the bolt head pushes the front sprocket forward and tightens the track.

It is impossible to steer a tank like an automobile because the tracks cannot be swivelled relative to the body of the tank. Instead, it is necessary to drive the track on one side faster than the track on the other side. This makes one side of the vehicle move forward faster than the other side, causing the tank to slither round and skid the front and rear ends of the tracks sideways over the ground. On soft ground this manoeuvre causes no difficulties and works successfully even on hard road surfaces.

In 1915, the first armoured fighting vehicles were being designed in Great Britain. The idea was so secret that a story had to be invented to disguise what was really going on. When the sheet steel material was being ordered for the armour plate of the first of the new weapons, all the correspondence said that it was needed for building "tanks". The name has stuck, and ever since then it is

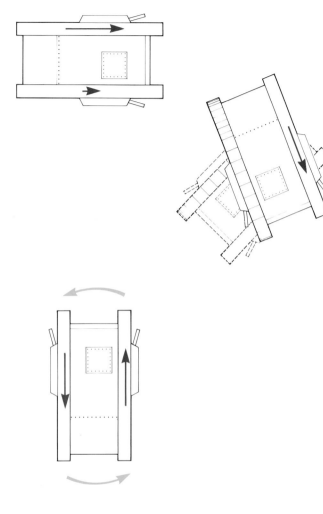

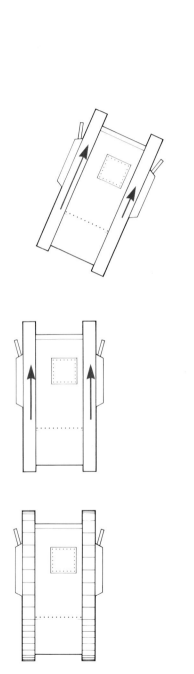

The tracks of a tank cannot be steered in the same way as the wheels of a car. In order to make a tank turn it is necessary to drive the tracks faster on one side than on the other. The tank then slithers the front and rear ends of its tracks sideways over the ground as shown in the diagram.

usual to refer to armoured fighting vehicles as tanks.

The early tanks had petrol engines of only 150hp. They were very slow, having a maximum speed of only about 6.5km/h (4mph) which is not much faster than walking pace. They had a six-pounder gun mounted in a turret on each side, but although they were so crude, the first tanks proved to be very effective, mainly because they terrified the enemy soldiers who had no idea how to stop them. They were not affected by rifle or machine-gun fire; a direct hit from an artillery shell would disable them, but most guns at that time could not be depressed low enough to engage them at short range. Most of the problems in action were caused by the poor reliability of the early tanks. They would break down due to some mechanical problem more often than they were damaged by enemy action.

The guns in the side turrets of the early tanks had only a very limited field of fire. It was, therefore, necessary to turn the whole tank round to point in the right direction to aim the guns. As mentioned earlier, it was not as easy to steer a tank on its caterpillar tracks as a conventional vehicle could be steered by turning its wheels. This limited the usefulness of the tank to an unacceptable degree and some better way of rotating the gun mounting had to be found.

Most later tanks have the main armament, usually a large calibre gun, mounted in a turret on the top of the chassis. The turret can be rotated through a complete circle and can fire at enemy forces no matter where they are relative to the tank's position. The turret with the gun and its ammunition has to be supported on a large circular bearing ring, with a mechanism to rotate the turret to

This example of an early tank now stands in a museum at Bovingdon in England. The restricted angle of fire of the guns in the side turrets is very obvious. Although by modern standards such tanks were very crude, they were successful mainly because of the element of surprise when they first appeared on the battle front in France.

One of the most widely used tanks of World War II was the M3 "Lee", seen here crossing a river. Although its profile is very high by today's standards, it successfully took part in many battles.

The M4 "Sherman" was one of the most famous American tanks of World War II. Fitted with a heavy calibre gun, it gave a good account of itself against the heavier tanks of the German Army.

Opposite top: Modern tanks are able to ford safely significant depths of water using a snorkel-type device either when crossing rivers or disembarking from tank landing vessels. Here we see an M60 with its hull almost submerged.

Opposite bottom: The main features of modern tank design are common to all the armies of the World. This diagram shows a T34/76 tank of the Soviet Red Army.

Below: This photograph taken during World War II shows a line-up of "Matilda" Mk.II tanks preparing to engage the Germans of Rommel's North Africa Corps.

the required direction. This ring and the bearings have to resist the strong forces resulting from the recoil of the gun. They therefore form a heavy item in the structure of the tank.

Despite their defects, the success of the first tanks soon led to their development in other countries. It also led to the design of anti-tank defence systems and the manufacture of means of engaging tanks and destroying them before they could do any damage. Guns were modified or specially produced for attacking tanks.

As a result, the armour plating of the tanks was made thicker so that they could resist direct hits from artillery shells. This had a disadvantage in that it made the tanks heavier, which meant they were slower and less able to manoeuvre. Consequently it became necessary to fit bigger engines to regain the speed which had been lost. Once again, more powerful engines naturally turned out to be heavier because the extra power could only be

obtained by increasing the size of the engine.

However thick the armour plating of a tank might be, a larger gun would still penetrate that armour. Armaments manufacturers were aware of this trend, with the result that more heavily armoured tanks led to the development of even bigger guns to attack them; a game of leapfrog between guns and armour which is still going on today. With the continuing development of new types of anti-tank weapons it has become even more difficult to design tanks which can survive in modern battle conditions.

World War II saw tanks being used in ways similar to those previously employed by navies with their fighting ships. Tanks were still used against fixed ground defences but engagements also took place between fleets of tanks. This happened especially in the deserts of North Africa where large numbers of tanks would advance into enemy territory. Because of the nature of the terrain, there were no natural obstacles in the landscape.

One of the shortcomings of tanks is that they find it difficult to cross rivers or canals and cannot cross mountain ranges except by way of already existing passes. In such types of territory it is relatively easy for the defending forces to know the routes which the invading tanks will take, because often they have very little choice. The defenders can, therefore, set up anti-tank weapons at the places where the tanks will be compelled to go.

In the desert, the situation was entirely different. To the tank the desert was like the ocean to a ship. It could travel in any direction without concern for the physical features. When it was known that a force of enemy tanks was advancing across the desert, an equal or greater number of

tanks would be sent out to engage them. Each side would be trying to knock out as many of the opposing tanks as possible and success would depend on a number of factors:

the number of tanks on each side;
the size of the guns which they carried;
the thickness of the armour which protected them.

There were obviously other factors involved, such as the tactics used by the commanders, the reliability of the tanks under battle conditions and the skill and determination of the tank crews. But, in general, the side which had the most tanks with the best armament came away with the victory. Many lessons about the best way to use tanks were learnt by military commanders during the Desert War and those lessons are still being applied today in the design of tanks and anti-tank weapons.

The most vulnerable part of a tank is its underbelly. Because it is not likely to be hit by gunfire it is usually made of thinner material. This makes it very prone to damage from explosions produced by anti-tank mines. The photograph shows the underside of a British tank of World War I.

Weaponry and Ammunition

To knock an armoured fighting vehicle out of action it is necessary to pierce its armour in order to disable the crew or to do so much damage to the driving system that the tank is brought to a standstill. The drive system, and particularly the tracks, are most easily wrecked by mines planted in the ground over which the tank is going to move. The underbelly of a tank is also more lightly armoured than its sides so that a mine may be able to distort the floor upwards, injuring the crew or the drive mechanism.

The problem with mine-laying is that the mines must be placed so that the tank drives over them and compresses them with its tracks. If the intention is to block a narrow pass to tanks, mines can be useful because, as we have already noted, the tanks have little choice about where they can go. If the mines are carefully sited, the tanks can hardly avoid running over them.

However, in the open field, tanks are best attacked by guns or guided missiles

The design of some modern tanks sacrifices armour for lightness in an effort to gain more speed and manoeuvrability. They can then be used against heavier tanks in the same way that fighter aircraft are used against bombers. The photograph shows a Kurassier tank destroyer.

which have the power to burst through their armour plate. Large fields of anti-tank mines were laid in the desert in World War II but the number of mines required was enormous. Tanks were also fitted with rotating shafts in front of them. Attached to the shaft was a large number of long chains. As the shaft rotated, the chains beat the ground in front of the tank, exploding any mines which lay in its path. When equipped with this device, tanks could drive straight across a minefield without being disabled.

The alternative to the use of mines to destroy or disable tanks is a direct attack on the hull of the tank using heavy guns or guided missiles. There are basically two ways of piercing the armour of a tank. One is by the use of kinetic energy, the other by the direct use of chemical energy.

Kinetic energy is the energy which a moving body possesses because of the speed at which it is travelling. The amount of energy increases as the square of the speed. If a stone is thrown at a window, it will bounce off if the stone is small or if it is thrown at too low a speed. If a bigger stone is thrown, or the small stone thrown at a higher speed, it will break the glass.

If a projectile can be fired from a gun at twice the speed, it will have four times the kinetic energy and, hence, four times the power to pierce the armour of an enemy tank. The kinetic energy is also proportional to the mass of the moving body. That is, a projectile which is twice as heavy will have twice the power to penetrate armour plate.

If a projectile has enough kinetic energy it will burst through the armour. In the confined quarters of a tank it will then ricochet around in the crew compartment, causing severe injuries if not death. It may also cause the ammunition stored in the tank to explode, with disastrous effects on the vehicle and its crew. If the projectile does not have enough kinetic

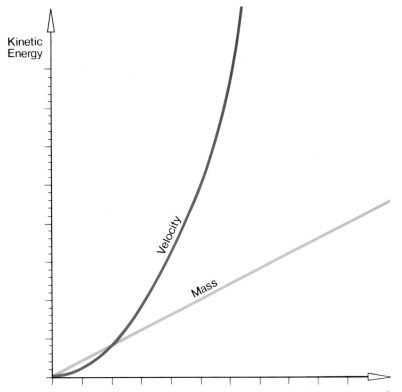

Kinetic Energy

Velocity

Mass

The ability of a shot to pierce an armour plate depends on its kinetic energy. As these diagrams illustrate, the kinetic energy is directly proportional to the weight of the shot but increases as the square of the velocity.

energy, it will rebound off the armour and be wasted without doing any significant harm.

As has been demonstrated, the way to increase the kinetic energy of a shell or a bullet is to make it heavier or to make it move faster. There is an added advantage in making it move faster. The target is moving during the time between the instant when the projectile is fired and when it arrives at the target. Therefore the quicker the projectile is travelling, the greater is the chance of hitting the tank at the exact point which produces the most damage.

Increasing the velocity at which a shell leaves the barrel of a gun involves major changes to the design of the gun. Longer barrels will result in higher exit velocities if the propellant charge can provide the extra energy needed to force the shell along the additional length of barrel, but the resulting gun is heavier and more difficult to handle.

The mass of the projectile can also be increased by making the bore of the gun larger, that is, by increasing the calibre. Once again, this involves large increases in the size and mass of the gun which entails other difficulties in fitting the gun and its ammunition into a tank of a given size.

It is probable that the guns mounted in today's tanks are as large as they will ever be. Other ways have been found of increasing the ability of projectiles to penetrate the armour of enemy tanks. One of these is known as the armour-piercing discarding sabot (APDS). In this case, the projectile is small in comparison to the bore of the gun barrel. To make it fit into the barrel it is surrounded by a jacket of light material, known as a sabot. As the shot leaves the barrel of the gun, the sabot breaks up and is discarded. As a result, all the energy released by the explosion of the propelling charge is transferred into the relatively light projectile, which travels at a very high velocity. The projectile is made of a very hard alloy so that it does not flatten as it hits the target. Instead it bores a hole in the armour plate and reaches the inside of the tank.

Armour-piercing projectiles can be made heavier without increasing their size by making them of heavier alloys. This has the advantage of making it unnecessary to increase the calibre of the gun. The heaviest of all metals is uranium, and depleted uranium has been used for the manufacture of anti-tank ammunition.

The accuracy of its gun is the main factor in determining how effective an armoured vehicle is going to be in combat, and increasing the muzzle velocity of the projectile is one way of increasing the accuracy of the gun. More recently,

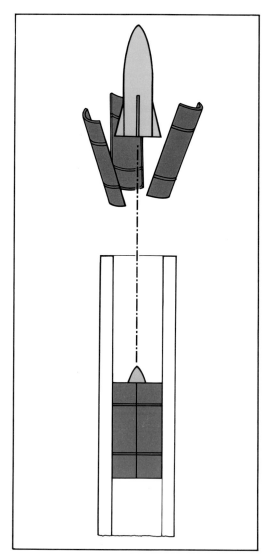

ammunition which is stabilized in flight by fins has been successful in obtaining much improved accuracy. The standard type of ammunition is stabilized in flight because it is rotating about its axis as it leaves the muzzle of the gun. The inside of the gun barrel has a series of spiral grooves running along inside it. The technical name for the grooves is "rifling". That is why the first hand-guns to be treated in this way were known as "rifles". A collar on the base of the shell engages in these grooves. As the shell is propelled up the barrel, the grooves compel the body of the shell to rotate very rapidly. After it has left the muzzle of the gun, the shell then acts like a gyroscope, stabilizing itself in flight and ensuring that it stays on its intended course.

One problem is that the rifling soon wears out because of the huge loads imposed on it each time the gun is fired. It also has to work in a very hot environment, subjected to the gases produced by the explosion of the propellant charge. The advantage of fin-stabilized ammunition is that it can be fired from guns whose

Left: If a shot is surrounded by a lightweight sabot, the pressure from the explosion of the propellent charge acts on a lighter mass and thus accelerates the shot more rapidly out of the barrel. As soon as the shot emerges from the muzzle, the sabot is discarded and the shot carries on to the target at high velocity.

Below: The modern anti-tank gun is capable of firing a high-velocity armour piercing shot which will penetrate the armour of an enemy tank. The gun shown here is a Soviet T-12 gun with a calibre of 100mm.

barrels are not rifled. The loss of accuracy due to the lack of spin is compensated by the guidance provided by the fins, which act in the same way as the fins of an aircraft.

The ammunition described so far depends on its kinetic energy for its ability to penetrate the armour of an enemy tank. The other type of ammunition depends on chemical energy for its effect. CE rounds, as they are known for short, do not depend on having a high velocity for their effectiveness but contain a specially designed explosive charge which is used to penetrate the armour plate of a tank.

There are basically two types of CE rounds. The first is known as a High-Explosive Squash Head (HESH). The shell has a soft casing so that on impact it spreads out as it hits the surface of the target. A fuse then detonates the charge which causes fragments of the armour plate to fly off on the inside of the enemy tank. This process is known as "spalling". The intention is to kill or seriously injure the crew or possibly to detonate the ammunition carried inside the tank. In either case, the tank will be immobilized.

The second type of CE ammunition is the High-Explosive Anti-Tank (HEAT) round. In this case the high-explosive charge itself is shaped so that its front is hollowed out, leaving a conical space. This is defined as a shaped charge. It is

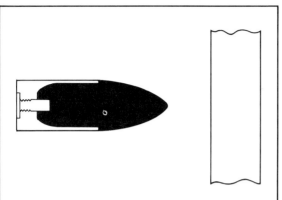

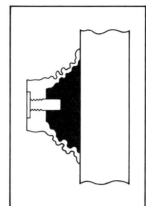

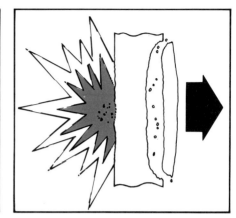

designed to explode at exactly the right distance from the armour plate. For this purpose, the fuse is activated by a rod of a carefully calculated length sticking out in front of the charge. The charge explodes when the tip of the rod touches the target. When the charge is detonated at the right distance from the target, the shape of the front surface of the charge focuses the force of the explosion very accurately at one point on the surface of the enemy tank. A relatively thin stream of hot gas travelling at very high speed cuts its way through the armour into the interior of the tank. HEAT rounds can be used in anti-tank armament which are less accurate than guns. These include rocket-propelled anti-tank projectiles launched by soldiers on the ground and anti-tank missiles launched from aircraft.

Some ammunition combines the advantages of both the kinetic-energy and the chemical-energy weapons. This is known as High-Explosive Piercing (HEP) ammunition. In this case, the round pierces the armour in the same way as a kinetic energy round but then a charge explodes inside the tank like a chemical energy round.

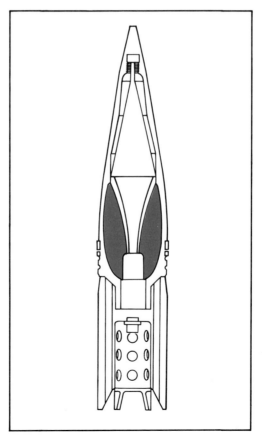

Above: A Squash Head anti-tank charge penetrates armour plate by the means shown here. On impact the charge spreads out over the plate before exploding. As a result fragments of plate are detached from the inside. These fly around at high velocity inside the tank.

Left: A section through a HEAT round explains the principle on which the shaped explosive charge works. The charge, shown shaded in the diagram, acts as a kind of lens focusing the blast at one point. The charge explodes at exactly the correct distance from the plate so that the force is concentrated in one spot. The hot gases produced by the explosion pierce the armour plate and penetrate to the soft interior of the tank.

Armour

The only justification for the use of any tank is that it is armoured. In action, it is going to be attacked by the enemy using gun-fire or guided missiles. To prevent its being knocked out of the battle, it must have armour plate of sufficient shape and thickness to protect it against all that the enemy can throw at it.

The original tanks of World War I relied on fairly thin steel plates to protect them. In the main they were only going to be attacked with rifle and machine-gun fire so that there was no need for anything more than a moderate thickness of armour which would be enough to stop small calibre ammunition. As tanks developed, however, battles between them became a regular feature of warfare, and

The French AMX-10 depicted here shows another approach to producing a tank destroyer. In this case a heavy calibre primary armament has been installed on the chassis of an existing armoured personnel carrier.

today's tank designers have to ensure that the enemy fire cannot penetrate the armour of the designer's own tanks.

Basically there are two ways of doing this. One is to make the armour plate so thick that the enemy fire is just not powerful enough to penetrate it. The other is to shape the armour in such a way that the enemy shot hits a sloping surface and is deflected off without breaking through. That is a good way of resisting armour-piercing rounds but it does not work so successfully with CE rounds. They do not have to hit square to the surface in order to penetrate the armour of enemy tanks.

Armour plate is usually made of special alloys of steel which have great hardness. They must not be too brittle though or they will flake on the inside when a shell explodes against them. This would be dangerous for the tank crew as fragments of the armour plate would fly off and hit them.

The obvious problem with armour plate is that it is very heavy. In a tank battle, speed and agility are very definite advantages to any tank lucky enough to possess those qualities. A great deal of effort has gone into the search for better forms of armour plate which are as strong as the solid type but lighter.

One solution to the problem of weight is to have not one piece of thick armour but two thinner plates with a gap in between them. In the case of CE ammunition the outer plate causes the round to explode at the correct distance but the inner plate is not at the focal point of the explosion. The inner layer of armour thus survives the attack undamaged. This design of armour is effective against HEAT and HESH rounds. Using the same principle, many tanks have curtains of plates hanging outside the tracks at the side of the vehicle. These cause the CE rounds to explode while they are still far enough from the body of the tank to cause minimal damage.

Many of the latest developments in the design of tank armour are still secret for obvious reasons. The so-called "Chobham armour", which was developed in Great Britain, uses a combination of different materials to absorb the impact of both kinetic-energy rounds and chemical-energy rounds. It is believed that the Chobham armour is made up from layers of steel, aluminium and ceramic materials arranged so that there are spaces between some of the layers.

One of the difficulties with compound armour is that it can only be made in flat sheets, making it impossible to produce nicely rounded shapes such as the ideal gun turret. The traditional rounded shapes for gun turrets are very effective in causing projectiles to ricochet off. Another problem is that where the flat plates meet there are bound to be sharp edges which form a weak point in the armour. Sharp edges also make it easier for the enemy to detect the tank.

From what has already been explained, it is obvious that the tank designer does not have an easy task in deciding on the best layout and armament for his next tank. What is needed is the right combination of size, weight, speed, guns and armour plate to give the best chance of survival in modern battle conditions. A review of the tanks at present in service with the armies of the world will quickly show that there is no one unique solution to the problem. No two countries agree about the design of tank which best fits the requirements, because the strategic needs of countries, differ so greatly.

The M1 Abrams Battle Tank

The search for the next battle tank for the US Army extended over a number of years. The need for an improved tank was made known in the late 1960s. At that time, an agreement was reached with the government of West Germany to cooperate in the design of a new tank for use by both countries. Because of difficulties with the organization of the project, the idea was abandoned in 1970.

It was then agreed that the United States and Germany would each develop their own tanks. The US efforts resulted in the XM-803 tank but this was not supported by the US Congress and funding was stopped in November 1971. It was thought that the design was too complicated and too expensive.

These political manoeuvres did not reduce the need of the US Army for a more modern tank. Early in 1972, work started on a design to a new specification issued by the US Army. Two companies, Chrysler and General Motors, were given contracts to design and build prototypes for evaluation by the Army.

Right: This photograph shows one of the 11 pre-production M1 tanks built by Chrysler for the trials which confirmed its capabilities and resulted in large orders being given to its manufacturers.

Above right: The unsuccessful General Motors submission for the M1 design competition is seen in this photograph taken during evaluation trials.

Opposite: An M1 Abrams battle tank speeds into action with its gun at the ready.

The need for efficient air filters to clean the air taken into the engine and the crew compartment is emphasized by this view of an M1 tank at speed. The tracks throw up a thick cloud of dust which would damage the engine if it were not filtered out in the intakes.

The requirements placed on the designers were very demanding. The tank obviously had to have better chances of survival in war than previous designs. Great attention had to be devoted to protection for the crew, safe stowage of the ammunition to prevent its being exploded by enemy fire, and the ability of the various systems to continue to operate successfully under combat conditions.

A high standard of performance was called for with regard to speed and manoeuvrability on rough ground. Particular attention was to be devoted to having an effective braking system. The tank had to be agile, that is, it had to be able to accelerate and slow down rapidly as the battle conditions might require. The armament specified included one main gun and two machine-guns, one for use against attacking aircraft.

An important requirement in the design specification was the need to provide protection for the crew from nuclear, biological and chemical warfare. This placed severe demands on the design of the ventilation system for the interior of the tank.

In addition to its operational requirements, the tank was required to satisfy cost targets, the most important of these being the cost of manufacture in the first place. The vehicle also had to survive with the minimum of maintenance in the field. This was partly because it costs a great deal of money to have trained personnel capable of servicing a tank on the battlefield. Also, it was unacceptable to have tanks out of action during a battle due to a lack of reliability in some item of equipment. Any faults which might occur during the life of the tank had to be easy to identify so that they could be corrected with as little delay as possible.

Finally, the tank had to have the potential for further development. As the science of warfare would undoubtedly produce new threats over the next few years, the tank would have to be modified to meet them. Such future developments had to be allowed for in the original design.

By the beginning of 1976, both companies had prototypes ready for comparative trials. One unconventional aspect of the Chrysler design was that it was powered by a gas turbine engine. All previous tanks had used piston engines. By November 1976, on the basis of the trials which had been carried out, the US Department of Defense decided to choose the Chrysler version of the new tank for future production. Chrysler were given a contract to build 11 pre-production tanks for further testing. By July 1978, the tanks were ready for trials.

The trials subjected the tanks to the worst conditions of warfare over the most inhospitable ground. The results of these trials showed the need for some minor changes to the initial design. The tracks had to be modified because their life was insufficient before they wore out. The air cleaners required some rethinking as there was no previous experience with the design of air cleaners for gas turbine engines under the conditions in which tanks are required to operate. One of the problems with gas turbine engines is that they require much more air than piston engines. In fact, they use about three times as much air as a piston engine of the same horsepower.

The air on a battlefield is dusty and dirty. It has to be filtered to remove the dust before it can be fed into the engine where it is mixed with fuel and burnt. Gas turbine engines have to be provided with

much larger air cleaners so that they can have available to them the extra clean air which they need to operate. The cleaners also have to be able to survive attacks using napalm which would burn them out if they were not specially designed to resist the heat. The air intakes have to be positioned on the body of the tank so that they do not suck in air from the surrounding dusty areas. This aspect also needs careful consideration before a decision on the final arrangement is reached.

On earlier tanks it was usual for the engine air to be taken in from the crew

The M1 Abrams battle tank is intended to counter the threat imposed by the Soviet T-72 tanks shown in this picture. The turret of the Russian tank is seen to be more rounded than that of the M1.

Opposite: This view of an M1 at speed shows the vehicle's secondary armament to advantage. The commander's position, to the left in this picture, mounts a 0.50in calibre heavy machine gun while the loader's weapon is a lighter 7.62mm machine gun.

compartment. This ensured a continuous flow of air through the crew's quarters. Today, it is necessary to protect the crew from attack by nerve gases and other chemical weapons. The use of nuclear weapons on the battlefield will result in radiation hazards if the air is taken directly into the crew compartment. For these reasons, the supply of air to the engines on the latest tanks is fed from the outside straight into the engines by way of the air cleaners. The air for the crew is treated separately to minimize the risk to them from chemical weapons and nuclear radiation.

In the end, the problems highlighted by the trials were overcome. In May 1978,

the design of the XM1, as the new vehicle was to be known, was approved and an initial order for 110 tanks was given to Chrysler. The first production vehicles were handed over to the US Army in February 1980 and the new tank entered service at the end of the same year. The intention had been to build 3,312 of the M1 tanks. However, at the end of 1978, it had already been decided to increase this number to 7,058 to counterbalance the number of Russian T72 tanks being built.

Despite its great size the M1 has a very low profile. If a tank is going to be hit by an enemy shell or missile, the most likely part to be hit is the turret. A well-designed tank will, therefore, keep the

turret as shallow as possible. The designers of the M1 have succeeded in this important aspect, which should make an important contribution to its chances of survival under war conditions.

The M1 weighs about 54.5 tons, the equivalent of more than 50 private automobiles. Most of that weight consists of the heavy armour which protects it against enemy attack. Despite its great

weight, the pressure which its tracks exert on the ground is only 0.93kg/cm^2 (13lb/sq in). This is because the tracks cover 5.85m^2 (63sq ft) of ground when the M1 is travelling over level country.

There are seven road wheels on each side, running across the upper surface of the lower half of the track. All of these wheels are sprung by steel torsion bars. That means that as the wheel moves upwards it twists a steel bar which absorbs the shock due to the vertical load on the wheel. At each of the front and rear ends of the tracks there is a toothed wheel, known as a sprocket. The rear sprockets are driven by the engine which

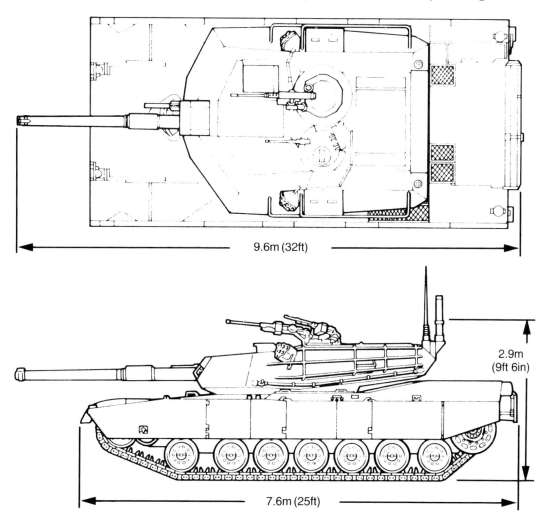

The main features of the M1 Abrams tank are given in this general arrangement drawing. Because of its good proportions it is easy to underestimate the size of the tank.

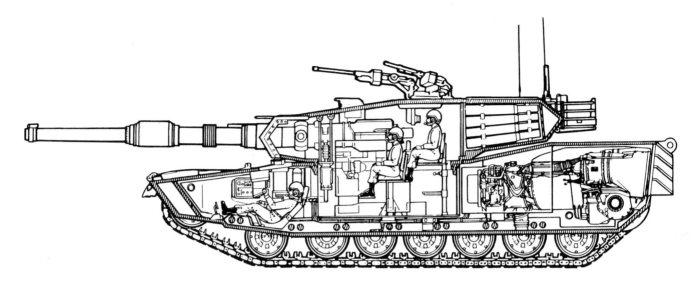

This cut-away view shows the internal arrangement of the M1 tank. The driver lies almost flat in the nose so as to reduce the height of the hull. The commander and the gunner are located in the turret. The loader is not shown, but he sits sideways near to the breech of the gun. Shells can be seen stored in the back of the turret. The engine is back at the rear, close to the sprockets which drive the tracks.

provides the motive power for the tank. The tracks themselves are completely shod with rubber.

The agility of the M1 is demonstrated by the fact that it can climb over obstacles up to 1.2m (4ft) high. Because of the length of its tracks, it remains stable when crossing the most uneven ground. It can even cross a ditch 2.7m (9ft) wide without falling in.

The length of the hull is 7.9m (26ft). The overall length including the barrel of the gun is 9.6m (32ft).

For its size, the M1 is not as high as might be expected. Its width is just 3.6m (12ft) and the designers have managed to keep its overall height down to 2.9m (9ft 6in), making it much less vulnerable to gunfire.

This reduction in its height has been achieved by careful design of the driver's position. Instead of sitting upright, the driver lies on his back with his head tilted forward. This arrangement makes possible a considerable reduction in the depth

of the hull and lessens the overall height of the vehicle.

The engine is a Lycoming ACT-1500C gas turbine. It can output 1,500hp when it is turning over at a speed of 22,500 revolutions per minute.

An armoured fighting vehicle would hardly be expected to match an automobile for speed. It is surprising, therefore, to learn that the maximum speed of the M1 on level ground is 72km/h (45mph). That is a very respectable speed for a vehicle which weighs over 50 tons. It can accelerate from rest to 32km/h (20mph) in only 6 seconds, and carries enough fuel to last it for over 480km (nearly 300 miles) without having to refill its fuel tanks.

The M1 needs a crew of four men to operate it. These include the commander, a gunner, a loader and a driver. The duties of the driver are obvious. The commander is in charge of the tank and the rest of the crew obey his orders. He decides where to go, which targets to

attack and which type of ammunition should be used. The gunner uses very cleverly designed equipment to detect the enemy, to measure how far away he is and to aim the gun so as to destroy his target. The loader feeds fresh ammunition into the gun after each round is fired.

Different types of ammunition are carried which are selected by the commander depending on the target under attack. The rounds available include all of those described earlier: armour-piercing discarding sabot (APDS), high-explosive anti-tank (HEAT) and high-explosive

The Lycoming gas turbine which powers the M1 can output 1500hp. Unlike the engines of other tanks, it has no reciprocating parts but works like a jet engine.

squash head (HESH). In battle the tank carries 60 rounds in specially designed racks to make them easily accessible to the loader.

The standard gun fitted to the early M1s was a rifled gun with a calibre of 105mm (4.13in). Its barrel was about 5.5m (18ft) long and the whole gun, including the breech block, weighed over a ton. When it was fired the gun recoiled 30cm (1ft). Each of the shells which it fired weighed about 18kg (40lb).

Later trials showed the advantages of using a smooth-bore gun. As was mentioned earlier, the loss of accuracy due to the absence of rifling in the barrel can be compensated by using fin-stabilized ammunition. The gun which is being installed on later M1s is of German design and is being manufactured in the United States under licence. It is called the Rheinmetall gun and has a calibre of 120mm (4.72in). The smooth-bore gun weighs almost 2 tons. M1 tanks fitted with that gun are known as the M1A2.

In addition to the main gun described above, the M1 carries two machine guns on the top of its turret. One of these is intended to be used as an anti-aircraft gun, the other can be used by the commander to attack enemy troops or light vehicles. They are able to fire about 900 rounds per minute.

The amount of ammunition carried on board is about 12,000 rounds. The design of the ammunition storage is arranged so

Opposite: This photograph has been exactly timed to show the brilliant flash issuing from the muzzle of the barrel when the M1's gun is fired.

The German smooth-bore 120mm Rheinmetall gun is seen here installed in a Leopard II tank of the West German Army.

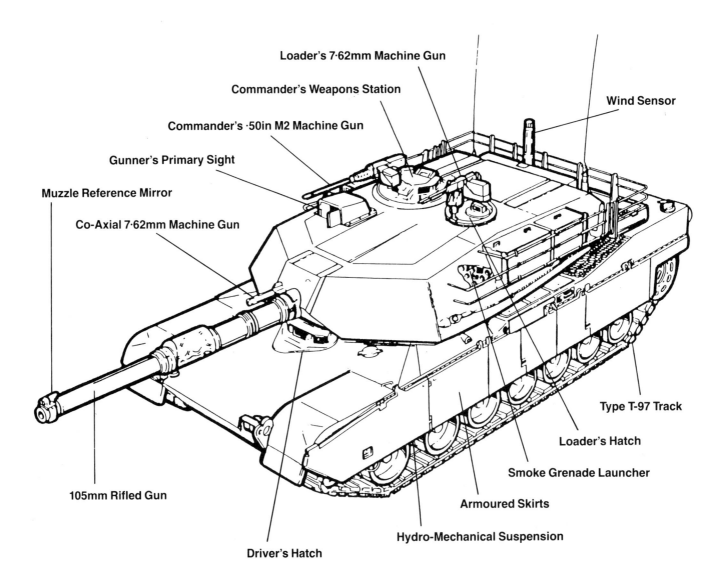

Loader's 7·62mm Machine Gun

Commander's Weapons Station

Commander's ·50in M2 Machine Gun

Gunner's Primary Sight

Muzzle Reference Mirror

Co-Axial 7·62mm Machine Gun

Wind Sensor

Type T-97 Track

Loader's Hatch

Smoke Grenade Launcher

Armoured Skirts

Hydro-Mechanical Suspension

Driver's Hatch

105mm Rifled Gun

as to minimize the danger of explosion due to enemy shot penetrating the body of the tank. In the M1, the ammunition is stored in a number of separate lockers distributed inside the hull. These lockers are provided with blow-off panels. If an enemy shell detonates in one of the lockers, a panel will blow out and allow the force of the explosion to be discharged outside the tank. Strong bulkheads between the lock-

ers also serve to prevent an explosion from making its way from one locker to the next. The access doors which separate the ammunition lockers from the crew are also strong enough to contain an explosion in any one locker and preserve the crew from serious injury.

In order to enhance its resistance to enemy fire, the M1 is protected by "Chobham armour". As explained earlier,

Opposite and above: By comparing the diagram opposite and the photograph above it is easy to identify the various items of equipment to be found on the hull of the M1 tank.

41

The ammunition
lockers in the M1 are
equipped with blow-off
panels. If an enemy
shot should hit the
stored ammunition
and explode it, the
pressure is relieved by
the panels blowing off.
Access doors separate
the crew from the
ammunition
compartment and
protect them from the
blast.

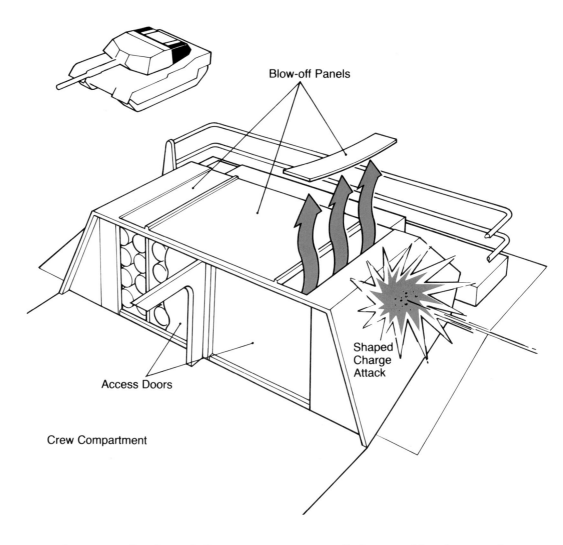

Blow-off Panels

Shaped
Charge
Attack

Access Doors

Crew Compartment

this achieves its effect by including spaces
within its thickness so that chemical-
energy rounds explode before they contact
the main armour.

When the tank is about to engage
an enemy, the range of the target is
measured by a neodymium YAG laser

range-finder, capable of measuring very
accurately the distance of objects up to
8km (5 miles) away.

The aiming of the main gun and the
timing of its firing are controlled by an
on-board digital computer. The computer
allows for the distance of the target, its

speed and the speed of the M1 when deciding the instant at which the gun should be fired to have the greatest chance of success. It also takes into account the weather conditions including the wind speed which is measured by a sensor at the rear of the turret.

The M1 can also lay smoke screens to confuse the enemy as to its exact position.

So that the M1 can engage in tank battles in the dark, it is fitted with a night-vision system. This detects the infra-red radiation given off by the target and presents an image on the commander's cathode ray tube. This process is called thermal imaging. The capabilities of the system are not public knowledge. It is believed that the commander has a clear view for a distance of at least 1.6km (1 mile) ahead of the vehicle even if the weather is such that normal visibility is very poor.

The range-finder on the right hand side of the turret enables the tank commander to measure exactly how far away an enemy tank is before he opens fire.

An interior shot of an
M1 battle tank's crew
compartment shows
how the available
space is fully occupied
by the crew and the
equipment. The
gunner sits ready for
action alongside the
breech of the gun.

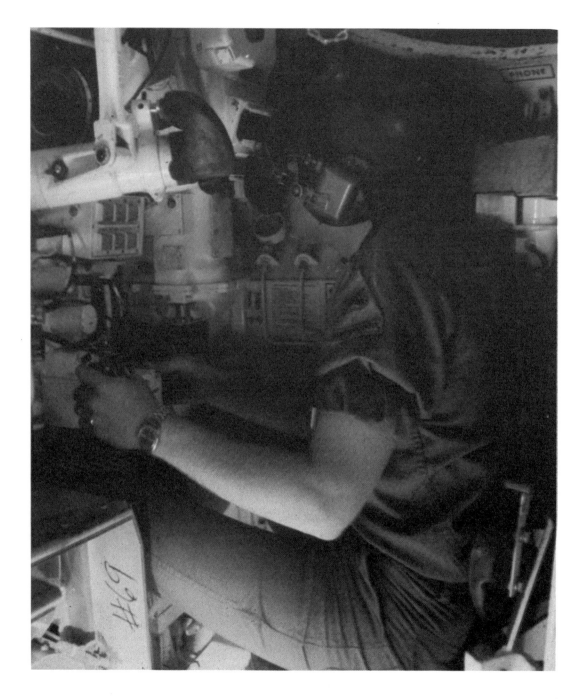

The M1 tank is obviously a very formidable fighting machine and so far has not been employed in anger in any conflict. At present it is only in service with the US Army, and ordered by, if not in service with, Egypt. It is to be earnestly hoped that it will never be necessary to use it in an all-out war. If such a day should come, however, the M1 will be able to attack enemy forces with the most powerful modern weapons. At the same time, it will be able to protect itself from enemy attack by its armour and by the design of its interior layout, which is intended to safeguard its crew against the worst that the enemy can throw at it.

45

Index

Figures in italics refer to captions

Agility, 36
Air filters, *28–32*
Air intakes, *30*, 31
Air supply to crew, 32
Ammunition, 17–21
  M1, 37–41
  storage, *36*, 39–40, *42*
AMX-10, *24*
Anti-tank guns, *18–19*
Anti-tank missiles
  Armbrust, *16*
  Lanze, *20*
Armament
  main, *38–9*
  secondary, *33*, 39
Armbrust, *16*
Armour, 14, *16–17*, 23–5
Armour-piercing
  discarding sabots
  (APDS), *18–19*
Armour-piercing
  projectiles, 17–18

Challenger, *23*
Chemical energy rounds,
  20–1, 25
Chobham armour, 25,
  41–2
Chrysler, 26–9
Compound armour, 25
Computer firing system,
  42–3

Crew, *36–7*
  compartment, *44*

Desert warfare, *14–15*
Design requirements, 29
Dimensions, 36

Engines
  early tanks, 12
  Lycoming ACT-1500C,
  29, *30*, 36–7

Features, *32–6*, *40–1*
Fin-stabilized
  ammunition, 19–20
Firing system, 42–3
First production M1s, 32

General Motors
  submission for M1, *26*
Gun turrets
  early *12*
  rotating, 12–13
Guns
  early, *12*
  M1, *33*, *38–9*

HEAT rounds, *21*, 25
High Explosive Piercing
  (HEP) ammunition,
  21

High Explosive Squash
  Head (HESH) charge,
  20–1, 25

Internal arrangement, *36*

Kinetic energy rounds,
  17–19
Kurassier, *17*

Lanze, *20*
Lee (M3), *13*
Leonardo da Vinci, 7
Leopard II, *39*
Lycoming ACT-1500C,
  29, *30*, 36–7

M3 Lee, *13*
M4 Sherman, *13*
M60, *15*
Machine guns, *33*, 39
Matilda Mk.II, *14*
Mines, 16–17

Night vision system, 43

Particulars, *32–6*, *40–1*
Pre-production tanks, *26*,
  29

Range-finder, *42–3*
Rheinmetall smooth-bore
  gun, 39

Sabots, *18–19*
Sherman (M4), *13*
Smoke screens, 43, *45*
Snorkels, *14*
Soviet tanks
  T-12, *19*
  T 34/76, *15*
  T-72, *32*
Speed, maximum, 36
Sprockets, 35–6
Squash Head (HESH),
  20–1

T-12, *19*
T 34/76, *15*
T-72, *32*
Tank destroyers, *17*, *24*
Technical features, *32–6*,
  40–1
Thermal imaging system,
  43
Tracks
  advantages, *8–10*
  M1, 29, *34*, 35, 36
  tensioning, *10*
Trench warfare, 7–8
Turret, 32–4

Weight, 34
Wheels, 35
WWI tanks, *7–12*, *16*
WWII tanks, *13–15*

XM-803, 26